The Herring Gull

The Herring Gull

By Karen O'Connor

DILLON PRESS
New York

Maxwell Macmillan Canada
Toronto

Maxwell Macmillan International
New York   Oxford   Singapore   Sydney

For my husband, Charles, who, with me, enjoys the beauty and companionship of the gulls along the beach near our home.

Acknowledgments

The author wishes to thank Amadeo Rea of the Museum of Natural History in San Diego, California, and Alan F. Poole and Doug Wechsler of the Academy of Natural Sciences of Philadelphia.

Photo Credits

Cover: O. S. Pettingill/VIREO
Back cover: A. Morris/VIREO
U.S. Fish and Wildlife Service: Glen Smart (title page); Jim Leupold (14-15).
VIREO: O. S. Pettingill (frontispiece); A. Morris (8, 11, 12, 18, 20, 37, 38, 41, 43, 46, 50, 53, 56); R. Cardillo (16, 28); R. Villani (23, 30); S. J. Lang (24); T. J. Ulrich (27); A. Carey (33); J. R. Woodward (35); R. Ricklefs (44).

Library of Congress Cataloging-in Pulication Data

O'Connor, Karen.
    The herring gull / Karen O'Connor.
        p. cm. — (Remarkable animals)
    Summary: Examines the physical characteristics, life cycle, and migration patterns of this adaptable bird, commonly known as the sea gull.
    ISBN 0-87518-506-1
    1. Herring gull—Juvenile literature. [1. Herring gulls. 2. Gulls.] I. Title. II. Series: Dillon remarkable animals book.
QL696.C46O26   1992
598' .338—dc20   91-40856

Dillon Press   Maxwell Macmillan Canada, Inc.
Macmillan Publishing Company   1200 Eglinton Avenue East
866 Third Avenue   Suite 200
New York, NY 10022   Don Mills, Ontario M3C 3N1

Macmillan Publishing Company is part of the Maxwell Communication Group of Companies.

First edition
Printed in the United States of America
10 9 8 7 6 5 4 3 2 1

Contents

Facts about
the Herring Gull

Scientific Name: *Larus argentatus*

Description:
Length—22.5 to 26 inches (57 to 66 centimeters)
Wingspan—4.5 feet (137 centimeters)
Weight—approximately 3 pounds (1.3 kilograms)
Physical Features—Heavy body; broad wings; square tail; long, stout bill that curves downward and ends in a hook
Color (Adults)—Silver-gray outer body with white underside; black wing tips with white spots; yellow bill with a tiny red spot

Distinctive Habits: Communicates with loud scream: *Chee! Chee! Chee! Kah! Kah! Kah!*; usually lives in large colony, or group; migrates about 1,000 miles, sometimes at speeds of 40 to 50 miles (64 to 80 kilometers) per hour

Food: Fish, garbage, worms, clams, insects, crabs, bird eggs, baby gulls, mice and other small mammals; also fruit and seeds

Reproductive Cycle: Individuals have one mate at a time, who may be a mate for life; females mature between 3 and 6 years of age; in summer, female lays three eggs, which take 26 to 32 days to hatch; males and females share the duties of raising the young

---

Life Span: About 10 years; one was known to have lived 28 years

Range: In the summer, the herring gull lives along ocean shores and lakes in Canada, New England, Europe, and northern Asia. In the winter, it can be found in a wide band across all of North America, Europe, Asia, and the North Atlantic and Pacific oceans

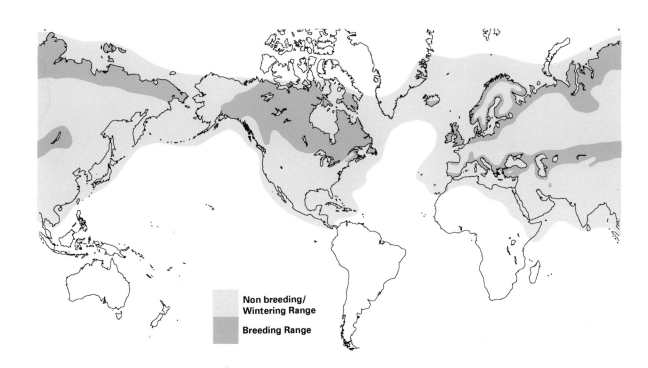

Non breeding/
Wintering Range

Breeding Range

Chapter 1

Life at the Top

Kah! Kah! Kah! The herring gull seems carefree as it glides gracefully through the morning sky. But this seabird is actually hard at work. Its eyes are fixed on the ocean below, looking for food.

Suddenly it beats its wings as hard as it can. The bird swoops down and races low over the water. Then it grabs a darting fish in its bill and soars into the sky.

The herring gull gets its name from the small fish, like herring, that it likes to eat. It does not limit itself to fish, however. Gulls probably enjoy a greater variety of food than any other animal—from buzzing insects, mice and moles, rats and cats, ducks, rabbits, shellfish, and worms to scraps of garbage. They also eat fruits, grains, and seeds. They will eat almost anything and everything they can swallow and digest.

The herring gull is the bird that people most often think of as a "sea gull." Unless you live near a lake or ocean, you may never have seen this handsome bird. In the United States, it is usually found along the Atlantic and Pacific coastlines and near some inland lakes.

Stout, Hooked Bill

One of the gull's most striking features is its long, stout bill. It curves downward and is shaped like a hook. The bird uses the curved bill to gather food on land and sea.

After a heavy storm, mollusks, starfish, and seaweed are washed ashore. Gulls use their special bills to prowl through the pile of fish and plants and pick out the most appealing bits of food. They also catch food in midair. Sometimes people on the seashore will toss small fish or bits of bread into the air. Then they watch as several gulls zoom in and pluck the treats before they hit the ground. Gulls can even snatch flying insects out of the air and eat them in midflight.

The herring gull uses its strong, hooked beak to gather food.

The herring gull also uses its strong bill to capture a clam or oyster. Then it flies high above the ground and drops it. When the shell hits a rock or pavement, it cracks open and the bird swoops down to pick up the raw shellfish. If the shell doesn't break the first time, the gull tries again. It may drop a clam a dozen times or more until it breaks.

Gulls prefer shellfish, but they can digest just about any kind of food.

Sometimes gulls find larger **prey***, like rats, young rabbits, or small birds. With several violent pecks of its bill, a gull will weaken or kill the animal before eating it.

The stout bill is not only used for catching and carrying food. It is also one of the body parts that makes it possible for the gull to live on both land and

*Words in **bold type** are explained in the glossary at the end of this book.

sea. Unlike most other animals, gulls can drink either fresh water or seawater. Animals generally do not drink seawater because they cannot pass the salt out of their bodies. But the gull has a pair of special **salt glands** above its eyes, which flush out the salt through openings in its bill.

Long Flight Wings

The herring gull is a model of streamlined flying. It can **glide** on currents of air for hours with its wings spread wide, feet neatly folded under its tail, and legs buried in its feathers. Or it can hang in one place for a long time, wings quickly fluttering, as it scans the sea and shore for food. This light movement is called **hovering**.

Long, narrow flight wings make gliding and hovering possible. Strong breast muscles move the gull's wings. These same muscles open and close the rib cage and empty and fill the lungs with air. This allows the bird to breathe and beat its wings at the same pace, so it will not tire out while hovering.

With its long flight feathers, the herring gull is a powerful and graceful flier.

The long flight feathers work like airplane propellers. They lift the bird and keep it in flight. Just as a pilot can change the angle of an airplane, the gull can change its slant by twisting the wing tips as the wings beat. The gull knows how to take advantage of the changes in airflow that create paths for gliding and hovering.

When the bird spots a fish or small animal, it is ready to swoop down, grab its prey, and soar away. The movements of its wings are similar to the ones your arms make when you row a boat. On the downstroke, the feathers on the wings lock together, creating a large surface that pushes against the air below. The gull moves forward by pushing the air

The movement of the wing tips propels the gull forward.

down and back with its powerful wings.

On the upstroke, the feathers separate like the slats in a window shutter. The wings move forward, curving slightly so air can flow over them easily. Air passes through the open feathers, making it easier for the wings to lift. At the top of the upstroke, the feathers lock together again.

16

Besides being expert fliers, gulls are also good swimmers, but they rarely dive into the water. They hunt for food along the surface, and when they spot something to eat, they swoop down to snatch it.

The gull's white underside and white wings blend in with the sky and make it hard for fish to see it. But the gull needs to act fast. If a fish is startled, it can dive out of reach. Then the gull must hover over the water once again until it spots another fish.

Wide Mouth and Expandable Gullet

The herring gull has a special mouth and throat that allow it to eat just about anything. It can swallow eggs, large fish, young birds, small rodents, and even steak bones without choking—thanks to its wide mouth and **expandable gullet**, a throat that stretches. In fact, it can swallow many things whole. If it catches a big fish, the gull can stretch its throat and swallow the entire meal in one gulp! A gull can also store large amounts of food in its body—as much as one-third its weight.

17

Because gulls eat both plants and animals, they are called **omnivorous**. They eat nearly anything. They also eat a lot. Gulls never turn down a free meal—even if it's somebody else's leftovers. They can often be seen following fishing boats, waiting for hours for food to be thrown overboard.

And while the herring gull may appear peaceful as it soars above the ocean, on the ground it can be a tough fighter. It frequently steals eggs from other birds or chases other gulls until they drop their prey. Gulls have even been known to peck another sea gull to death as they scramble to snatch its prey.

A stout, hooked beak, long, narrow flight wings, a large mouth, and an expandable gullet make the herring gull a hardy member of the bird family. And its ability to live near fresh or salt water and to digest just about anything helps this remarkable animal survive.

Its wide mouth and roomy throat allow
the gull to eat giant portions.

The herring gull is at home on the shores of both oceans and lakes.

Chapter 2

Winged Beach Bum

The herring gull is a natural beach bum! It spends most of its life picking at seaweed along the shore, rummaging through trash cans and garbage dumps, and soaring just above the water in search of food. This bird is well suited to life at the beach. It can swim as well as fly.

The Silvery Ravenous Seabird

To most people, the herring gull is simply a "sea gull." But to an **ornithologist**, a scientist who studies birds, the herring gull is known as *Larus argentatus* (LAHR-uhs ahr-jehn-TAH-tuhs). Scientists have an organized method of studying living things. They give each **organism** a two-part Latin or Greek name that usually describes its special features. No other animal has that name. As with humans, its first and last names give a clue to the animal's family and close relatives.

The herring gull's scientific name is part Greek and part Latin. The Greek word *Larus* means "a ravenous [extremely hungry] seabird." Most other gulls are also named *Larus*. The word *argentatus* is Latin for "silvery."

A Noisy Neighbor

It is easy to spot the "silvery ravenous seabird." Adult birds usually have silver-gray outer bodies, snow-white undersides, and black wing tips with white spots. Their legs and feet are pink. Their bills are yellow with a tiny red spot on the side. Males and females look alike, although the male is heavier and has a thicker beak.

The herring gull is one of the larger members of the gull family. It is a long-winged, web-footed water bird about twice the size of a crow. It measures 22.5 to 26 inches (57 to 66 centimeters) long and weighs

The "silvery ravenous seabird" is a hardy member of the gull family.

about 3 pounds (1.3 kilograms). During flight, its outstretched wings measure 4.5 feet (137 centimeters).

Herring gulls are big eaters, graceful fliers, strong fighters, and noisy neighbors. Their loud cries are sometimes harsh to human ears. A flock of yelping gulls can create quite a stir on the beach. Chances are these hungry birds are fighting about food.

Kah! Kah! Chee! Chee! Herring gulls yelp and

A gull's call can mean many things—hunger, warning, attack!

screech as they compete for a leftover picnic lunch. Gulls have a variety of other sounds too. A loud *kleew* from one herring gull is frequently answered by other gulls. Scientists do not know exactly what this common call means. They believe it may be a way the birds tell one another where other gulls are.

It seems that gulls can tell each other apart by

voice as well as, sometimes, by sight. Mates, especially, can recognize each other even from a distance away. They can also pick out their own chicks from among all the others in a group.

The sharp notes of a gull's trumpeting call sound an alarm that danger is near. The mournful mew is used during the mating season. And gulls use a sound described by one scientist as *huoh-huoh-huoh-huoh* while building their nests and during flights with other gulls.

What a racket the gulls make at their breeding grounds! Calls for mating, warning, hunger, attack, and begging create a mixture of loud and soft sounds. Only members of the gull family can understand and answer them.

Relatives around the World

Larus argentatus is most often seen in North America and northwestern Europe, but this **species**, or kind, of gull has relatives around the world. While the habits and behavior of most gulls are similar, there

are many differences in the plumage (feathers) of the various species. Some have black heads. Others have dark feather cloaks around their necks. Still others have brown or gray markings. A species of gull that lives in the Arctic has a pure white dress that blends in with its snow-covered surroundings.

The herring gull looks a lot like some other large gulls. Sometimes you can tell the species apart only by the color of their eyes. For instance, the glaucous gull's eyes have a yellow iris—the center of the eye— and a bright yellow eye ring. The herring gull also has a yellow iris, but its eye ring is orange.

The gull family contains a great many species. Twenty-nine of the forty-four known kinds live in the Northern Hemisphere of the world. In the United States alone, one gull species or another lives at least part of the year in every area of the country.

This dainty, red-billed gull is a relative of the herring gull.

Every year, herring gulls gather together in colonies, where they mate and rear their young.

Chapter 3

A Gathering of Gulls

The herring gull is a great traveler. You may see this bird darting for fish along the West Coast from Alaska to Mexico. Or you may notice it hunting for clams on the East Coast from Florida to the Arctic. Along both coastlines, you may spot this lively bird following boats and barges or searching the sands for insects and small plants. All this traveling is part of the gull's **migration cycle**.

Long-Distance Fliers

As the seasons change, the herring gull often flies long distances, or migrates, to live in climates with comfortable temperatures and good food supplies. Gulls can exist in cold climates, but only if there is plenty of food.

During their long flight south, gulls often stop at lakes to drink and bathe.

During the spring and summer, gulls need to be in a good place for **nesting** and raising their young. The best **breeding grounds** in North America extend from Alaska, across northern Canada, to the shores of the Atlantic. Gulls breed along eastern Canada, south along the New England shores, and inland around the Great Lakes. During the autumn and winter,

many flock to the southern United States.

Some gulls don't have to migrate. Those that live near areas with a large human population, for example, don't need to migrate because they can survive by **foraging** through garbage dumps.

But most gulls start leaving their winter homes in the south as spring approaches. Some fly 40 to 50 miles an hour for two or three days while migrating north. Others take their time, depending on the weather and the food supply along the way.

During the long flight, the gulls make several side trips inland for food. Some stay in the area around the Great Lakes in the midwestern United States. They wait until farmers prepare for spring planting. Then they feed on the insects and worms exposed by plowing. At night, they rest in flocks on lakes or sandbars.

Large numbers of birds are lost during such flights. Some birds, usually older ones, grow weak. They simply can't fly anymore. Others may lose their way in a fog. But most of the gulls know where they are going, and they land safely at their destination.

Organizing the Colony

Gulls live in large groups called **colonies**, and members often stay together for life. Every spring, each group returns to the same place as the year before.

Returning gulls yelp and scream as they organize their colony on a New England shore. This process takes place slowly, since not all the gulls arrive at once. And the ones that arrive first must take special precautions before they can settle down.

They have many enemies to guard against. Foxes, dogs, cats, and skunks, which like to steal eggs or carry off chicks, may be in the area. Gulls often nest on islands to avoid such ground **predators**. Some birds, like hawks, are dangerous, too, and they can swoop down without warning.

Gulls take great care to avoid such powerful predators. They approach their breeding ground carefully. They do not land immediately. First they fly in circles around the area, looking for intruders.

Powerful predators, like the bald eagle, can swoop down suddenly on unwary gulls.

They continue this inspection for several days. If no enemies are seen, one brave bird lands. This gull turns its head again and again, watching for danger. Then it joins the group and they fly away. When the birds return, they are ready to stay.

After they settle down in their breeding ground, the gulls must still watch for predators. When an enemy does wander in, the first gull to spot it sounds the alarm with a loud trumpeting call. Within seconds, the breeding ground is alive with flapping wings and loud screeching as the gulls take to the sky. Often they stay away until it is safe to return. Sometimes they try to scare off the predator by flying low over its head.

Setting up Territories

Although gulls are grouped in colonies, each mating couple lives within its own area, or **territory**. Territories are a fairly safe area where a pair can mate and raise a family. In order to keep out intruders, gulls have special ways of communicating. In addition to

Gulls use certain positions, or postures, as well as calls to
"speak" to one another.

their various calls, gulls "speak" to one another by
holding their bodies in different positions, or **postures**.

Because fighting is dangerous, gulls try to avoid
it. Postures can act as threats to keep other birds
away. Only when the threat fails do gulls actually

come to blows. The birds have several postures:

* *The upright threat posture.* Gulls fight with their bills and wings. In this position, the neck is stretched up and the bill pointed downward, ready to attack. The **carpal joint** of the wing—like the wrist on a human hand—is pushed forward. The gull is ready to beat its opponent with its wings.

* *Choking.* This is both a movement and a call. Two gulls bob their heads up and down and make deep sounds in their throats. They do this to warn off an intruder.

* *Grass-pulling.* Instead of fighting, an aggressive gull will face an opponent, peck violently at the ground, and pull out a beakful of grass. This is its way of letting off steam.

* *The anxiety posture.* A gull stretches its neck forward and flattens its wings against its body. From this position, it can escape if it needs to.

Gulls usually try to avoid fighting, but when necessary they can be fierce.

Two other positions—*hunched* and *facing away*—let gulls know that the performer is not threatening.

Once the gulls have organized their colony, they are ready to settle down to the business of mating, building their nests, laying their eggs, and raising their young.

Chapter 4

A Family Affair

Flap! Flap! Flap! Caw! Caw! Caw! Though it is late March, the air still holds the chill of winter in the herring gull's breeding ground along the coast of Maine. Green shoots begin to poke through the muddy soil. And streams and lakes begin to thaw as the sun melts their icy cover.

Courting, Mating, and Nesting

One female herring gull is ready to breed for the first time. She knows through **instinct** that she must find a mate. When she sees an available male, she walks toward him, leaning her head and body forward. She tosses her head and utters a soft "begging" call.

When he doesn't attack her, the female becomes more confident. She pushes him with her body and

A pair of courting gulls.

39

pecks at his bill. As she circles around him, the male tries to turn away from her. But she stays as close as possible.

Soon a swelling appears in the male's neck. He opens his mouth and coughs up some food. The female eats greedily. By feeding her, the male has accepted her as a mate. They are "engaged."

Their courtship will usually last for weeks. Sometimes, instead of feeding, the male and female will mate. For mating to be successful, both must take an active role. Each tosses its head and makes the soft "begging" call. Then the male flutters up on top of the female's back and brings his body into contact with hers at a place where his sperm can enter her reproductive canal. The sperm **fertilizes** the egg, and a new life begins.

Gulls will mate many times. Once they pair off, they will probably mate at the same breeding ground each year. Most herring gulls keep the same mate for life. But if its mate dies, a gull finds a new one almost immediately.

Most herring gulls choose one mate for life.

After mating, the male and female build their nest. They collect stems from dried weeds, bits of grass, and twigs for their new home.

The female sits on the nest and carefully arranges the nesting material around her body. She is busy indeed. But she is not only concerned with nest building—she appears interested in playing with her mate.

She nibbles at his neck and bill as if inviting him to dance. They face each other, stretch their necks, and lean their bodies forward. As they dance, they sing with a low-pitched gurgling sound.

Suddenly they are interrupted. A noisy male from the colony flies into their territory. *Peck! Peck! Peck!* The male is quick to defend his home and his mate. The female watches from a distance. Then suddenly she moves toward the intruder and pokes him forcefully. He flies off, and the pair resume their dance.

When she is ready, the female settles into the nest. It is time to lay her eggs. She lays three eggs, one every day or two. They vary in color from olive green to light blue to cinnamon, with brown, gray, or lilac markings. This coloring blends in with the surroundings and helps keep the eggs safe from predators.

The parents take turns **incubating**—or warming—the eggs. The female fluffs her feathers and sits down gently on the eggs while the male goes off to search for food. When he returns with juicy insects or

Parent gulls take turns warming the nest.

After a long, hard struggle, a chick emerges from its shell.

tasty fish, they change positions, and the female goes off to feed.

A Family of Five

The egg provides all the nourishment the developing gull needs. Inside each egg, a thick, clear liquid surrounds a yellow yolk with a single spot on it called

a **cell**. The single cell divides and becomes a group of cells. Over the course of the next 26 days, these cells gradually form parts of the bird's body. The tiny heart begins to beat. As the chick grows, it absorbs the yolk and the clear liquid. When they are nearly gone, the chick stretches and squirms within the crowded egg. It is time for it to hatch.

The chick chips a hole in the egg with a small, thornlike point called an egg tooth, located at the tip of its bill. It pecks, then rests, pecks, then rests. The bird isn't used to such hard work! After two or three hours of struggling—sometimes as many as ten—a tiny wet head pokes out of one end of the shell.

Soon two other chicks join the family. They are all covered with soft, fluffy feathers called "down." The parents are quick to warm the wriggling **hatchlings** until their wet feathers dry off.

By this time, the chicks are mighty hungry. They beg for food by pecking at the tiny red spot on the side of each of their parents' bills. The male or female then spits up food and feeds it to the downy chicks.

A pair of soft, downy chicks.

In and Out of the Nest

When their long feathers appear, the **nestlings**, or young gulls, spend a lot of time stretching and beating their wings. Soon they are able to rise into the air, leaping and flapping their wings at the same time. They also spend time watching their parents and other adult gulls fly and forage for food. After a few

weeks, they are ready to explore their surroundings on their own.

There is danger all around. Natural enemies like foxes are always on the lookout for small gulls. Other gulls in the colony will attack, too, if the chicks are unprotected.

When a predator is sighted, gulls give a loud trumpeting call. Chicks freeze where they are, or they find hiding places. When the danger is past, the parent gull will mew to its chicks that "all is well." Each chick recognizes its parents' voices and so can find them in the crowded colony.

By midsummer, the young gulls have become strong fliers. They are able to protect themselves from predators and are ready to join a flock of other young gulls.

Preening and Molting

In late summer, after the young have left the nest, the male and female have more time for themselves. They gather with other gulls along the shore and hunt small schools of herring and other fish.

As they must do every day of their lives, the gulls also use this time to **preen** their feathers. The female rubs her bill into a small oil sac under her tail. Then she carefully strokes her feathers with the oiled bill to smooth and waterproof them.

As the male preens, a feather falls to the ground, then another and another. He is beginning to **molt**. During the remaining summer months, the male and female will slowly shed their old coats. Strong, new pearl-gray feathers will replace the old worn-out ones. Now, with their thick undercoat of soft, down feathers to protect them against sleet, snow, and rain, the gulls are ready to begin their long journey south.

South for the Winter

In late autumn, it begins to get colder. The last leaves fall from the trees. Insects die. Crabs go deeper into the water and are harder to find. And fish and clams are often hidden under thin sheets of ice.

The male and female join other gulls for the long

journey to their winter home. After flying for several days across hundreds of miles, they reach a stretch of beach along the South Carolina shore. But they do not stay in one place. They wander from one spot to the next, searching for food near their winter homes. A location with plenty of food is more important to them than the place itself.

The male and female gradually separate during the winter months. Like other herring gulls, they spend their days feeding, preening, sleeping, and defending themselves from danger.

But they have not forgotten each other. As the first signs of spring appear, the male and female become restless. It is time once again to prepare for the flight north.

When they reach the familiar breeding grounds, the male and female recognize each other. And their courtship begins again.

Chapter 5

"No Hunting Allowed!"

Today hundreds of thousands of gulls soar above the Atlantic and Pacific coastlines. But less than a hundred years ago, herring gulls were nearly **extinct** along the North Atlantic coast. People had sold their eggs by the basketful. And hunters had shot thousands of them for their beautiful feathers, which were used to decorate ladies' hats. By the end of the 19th century, adult gulls were so rare that people bought them for 50 cents apiece, a considerable sum in those days.

In the 1890s, a group of people interested in the welfare of birds guarded some of the breeding colonies off the coast of Maine. During that time, the use of gull eggs and feathers decreased. In 1916, representatives from the United States and Canada signed

A hundred years ago, herring gulls were killed for their fine feathers.

an agreement for the protection of migratory birds. Today a federal law protects the gull. Killing any gull is punishable by a fine of up to $500 and six months in jail.

Gulls Today

During the last 70 years, the number of herring gulls has increased dramatically. Between one and two million populate the United States today.

Gulls in such great numbers are often considered pests. They swarm garbage dumps and trail after ships for hours. They also leave their droppings behind on lampposts, wharves, and boat docks. They even create safety problems at airports. Airplane engines can be damaged when the birds are sucked into them during takeoff and landing.

Before herring gulls were nearly wiped out at the end of the 19th century, overpopulation was not a problem. Natural enemies and starvation kept the gull population balanced. So why is there a problem now?

Because it can eat a wide variety of food, the herring gull can **adapt** to almost any condition. It is

Today, because people have created too much garbage, there are too many gulls.

a strong survivor—so strong that it can survive on the garbage, sewage, fish parts, and beach trash that our wasteful society spews out. The more people, the more waste. And the more waste, the more gulls.

The exploding gull population also endangers other birds. Terns and plovers, for instance, are threatened when gulls take over their nesting grounds or steal their eggs. Some naturalists suggest that such gulls be poisoned or shot to give endangered birds a chance to survive. Unfortunately, this type of wild-life management may be the only way we can keep some species alive in the next century.

But we cannot control the gull population as a whole by shooting at it. Gulls who are chased out of one area simply move to another. The key to gull population control is garbage control. Not until we figure out how to cut down on the amount of garbage we produce and find new ways to dispose of it will the herring gull problem be solved.

Gulls Yesterday and Tomorrow

In Salt Lake City, Utah, there is a monument, topped by two gold-plated gulls, which stands in honor of the bird that saved the town. Sea Gull Monument commemorates a time in 1848 when a flock of inland gulls devoured millions of grasshoppers that were plaguing the early settlers of the region. The ravenous birds saved the year's crops—and the

settlers were grateful.

The herring gull, raucous and beautiful, has lived side by side with human beings for a very long time. Like us, it has adapted well to the changing environment. It always seems to find something to eat and a way to survive. But if the herring gull is not to survive at the expense of other, less adaptable species, we must find a way to keep the environment safer for all animals. That way, when the herring gull flies over the shores of our continent, it will not fly alone.

Glossary

adapt—to adjust to changes in order to survive

breeding grounds—the location where gulls gather to mate and rear their young

carpal joint—a joint in the bird similar to the human wrist

cell—the smallest unit that forms all living things

colonies—groups of animals or plants of the same kind, living or growing together

expandable gullet—a stretchable throat

extinct (ehk-STINGKT)—no longer living anywhere on earth

fertilize (FURT-il-eyes)—to combine a sperm and an egg to begin the process that gives life to a new creature

forage—to hunt or search for

glide—to fly on currents of air without flapping the wings

hatchlings—creatures that have recently hatched from eggs

hovering—hanging in the air in one place, with quickly fluttering wings

incubating—warming eggs by sitting on them until they hatch

instinct (in-STINGKT)—a way of acting or feeling that an animal is born with and does not have to learn

migration cycle—the pattern birds follow to move with the changing seasons from one area to another for feeding or breeding

molt—to shed old feathers before they are replaced with new ones

nesting—to build and sit on a nest

nestlings—young birds that have not yet left the nest

omnivorous (om-NIV-er-es)—eating both animal and vegetable food

organism (OHR-guh-nihz-uhm)—a living thing

ornithologist (ohr-nuh-THAL-uh-jihst)—a scientist who studies birds

postures—ways of holding one's body

predator (PRED-uh-tuhr)—an animal that hunts other animals for food

preen—to clean and straighten feathers, using the beak

prey—an animal hunted for food by another animal

salt glands—the organs above the herring gull's eyes that flush out the salt from the seawater that the bird has drunk

species (SPEE-sheez)—a group of plants or animals that have certain characteristics in common

territory—a region or piece of land belonging to an individual or a group

Index

Karen O'Connor has enjoyed observing birds since she was a little girl. In recent years, she has become fascinated by seabirds. Ms. O'Connor and her husband like to watch them during daily walks along the beach near their home in San Diego, California.

Once an elementary-school teacher, Ms. O'Connor has been a free-lance writer for nearly 20 years. She is the author of more than 25 books for children and adults and has published numerous articles in children's magazines. The mother of three children, Ms. O'Connor has three grandchildren.

60